THE SOFT HOURS

THE SOFT HOURS

Poems

_____

LEO PIOTR

Ness House Press

Contents

morning

dawn light   3
piano practice   4
blueprints   5
mountain seeds   6
ghost stories   7
3 am   8
scattered light   9
glass hours   10
matches   11
morning coffee   12
on running   13
scars   14
conference room   15
garage   16
i burnt my hand   17
corner office   18
true north   19
cartography of departure   20
immigrant's inventory   22

afternoon

two tongues   27
corner store   28
tinder profile   29
d.o.m.s.   30
lunch break   31
soft names   32
two strengths   33
laundromat   35
between worlds   36
heritage   37
my office bathroom   38

siesta 39
the rules 40
old ways 41
lessons 42
between shifts 43
sunday afternoon 44
playing catch 45

evening
starved 49
sessions 50
on crying 51
the train ride 52
the artists' studio 53
the cat in a bowl 54
stage notes 55
undoing 56
a bridge 57
first date 58
peeling fruit 59
dinner table math 60
under the light 61
evening's prayer 62
tending flames 63
hello, ms patricia 65
circle 66
stoned-faced 67
bright, light, city 69

night
hospital waiting 73
surname 74
last train 75
night shift 76
gym mirror 77
closing time 78
worker's hands 79
i love her, still 80

permission   81
in my father's kitchen   82
conversations   83
a view from the roof   84
night prayer   85
strawberry   87
waiting   88
night mass   89
typing   90
gaming   91

About the Author   93

morning

dawn light

you sleep
like a poem
i'm afraid to write

while morning
traces maps
across your skin

i memorize
territories
i can
never own

piano practice

the neighbors

never complain

about music

that sounds like grief

blueprints

they said
"be a man"
but never gave me
the blueprints

so i drew my own
with trembling hands
and watercolor dreams

turns out
strength flows
in many directions
like spilled ink
flowing off a table

mountain seeds

planted in concrete

we grow anyway

through sidewalk cracks

and city grime

there is a mountain

inside my chest

where doubt once lived

i water it daily

with patience

ghost stories

they say

men don't feel

loss

my phone

holds graves

of conversations

that died mid-sentence

3 am

in the soft hours
between midnight and dawn
when the world stops
asking me to be stone

i let my shoulders drop
like autumn leaves
and remember how to breathe

the silence holds me
like my mother once did
before i learned
that boys don't cry

scattered light

i am the son
of autumn leaves and winter frost
carrying generations
of unspoken words
in my bones

when father taught me to build walls
he never mentioned how to tear them down

now i stand in scattered light
learning to be
strong autumn's shadows
and soft winter's fears

glass hours

i break
like crystal
in empty rooms

where no one
can hear
how masculinity
shatters

matches

mother always warned

about playing

with matches

but some lessons

we must learn

through burning

morning coffee

steam rising

from a ceramic cup

like prayers

to a gentler god

these quiet moments

before the world

demands its armor

i trace the rim

with careful fingers

learning to hold

delicate things

on running

sweat or tears

it doesn't matter

which falls

my body knows

both are ways

of letting go

scars

scars tell stories

purple-tongued lashes

on white,

morning skin

some marks

are worth

the flame

conference room

they book meetings

in hour blocks

but grief

keeps its own

schedule

between calls

i practice

looking strong

in empty corridors

garage

fixing broken things
was my father's
language for love

it's why
his hands shook red
when he couldn't
repair us

i burnt my hand

i burnt my hand

in a fire

you didn't pull me out

i burnt my hand

in a fire

because you

reached out

corner office

blinds

filter sunbeams

into prison bars

across my desk

and

even glass walls

can trap souls

true north

after enough
wrong turns
you learn

some roads
lead nowhere

cartography of departure

The day we left Warsaw, my mother packed history
into cardboard boxes smaller than our memories.
Grandmother stood at the window, her hands folded
like old maps no longer needed for navigation.

I was twelve, old enough to understand loss
but too young to hold its entire weight.
Suitcases spoke in whispers of things left behind:
the copper-tone church bells, grandfather's woodworking
tools,
the specific shade of light that used to fill our kitchen.

Toronto promised something else entirely—
a landscape of possibility and forgetting.

Each mile we traveled became another stitch pulling two
worlds apart, then together again.

My father's silence was a language all its own.

He counted kilometres like currency,

measuring the cost of a dream against

the weight of everything we could not bring.

At the border, I watched Poland shrink

in the rearview mirror—a photograph

growing smaller, its edges fraying.

Some roots, I learned, travel beneath the surface,

finding water in unexpected places.

immigrant's inventory

Let me count the things that crossed oceans with me:
One silver wedding ring (my mother's)
Three photographs of people who no longer exist
Except in memory and occasional dreams

A dictionary with pages worn soft from translation
Margins filled with words that have no equal:
Tęsknota — a homesickness so deep it aches
Żal — a sorrow that sits heavy in the chest
Resilience — the language I'm still learning

My accent is a map of journeys:
Consonants sharp as Warsaw winters
Vowels softened by Ontario summers

Each word a negotiation between what was

And what is becoming

I collect languages like some collect stones:

Polish of my childhood

English of my becoming

The silent language of migration

That lives between heartbeats

Some nights I wake speaking

In a tongue no one else understands

A conversation with ghosts

My dearest travel companions.

afternoon

two tongues
_____

my mother's language

sleeps

under my tongue

like honey

crystallized in winter

in meetings

i speak of metrics

and growth

while babcia's recipes

dissolve slowly

in my mouth

corner store

mrs. nowicki asks
why i don't visit
the old neighborhood
anymore

her eyes heavy
with the weight
of empty chairs
at sunday mass

i buy her pierogi
with plastic paper dollars
and swallow guilt
like communion

tinder profile

they want a man
who is strong
but never frightening

successful
but never busy

confident
but never proud

i edit myself
into smaller pieces
until the puzzle
fits their frame

d.o.m.s.

muscles aching
but it's not the weights
that make me strong

it's the way i've learned
to lay down my shield
in empty locker rooms
and whisper truths
to mirror-men
who finally
whisper
back

lunch break

watching pigeons
court each other
on concrete

how strange
to feel lonely
in daylight

soft names

in board rooms
i pronounce my name
the way they
prefer

soft edges
rounded vowels
nothing sharp
enough to catch

but at night
i whisper it properly
like a prayer
i almost forgot

two strengths

in the old country

strength was simple:

steady work

quiet prayer

vodka straight

here

they want warriors

who weep

giants

who bend

men

who speak feelings

in full sentences

. . .

it is learning

how to be

both granite

and water

laundromat

spin cycle hypnosis

powered

by a loonie

watching strangers'

lives tumble

into clean beginnings

between worlds

they call me
lucky
to have escaped

but
they don't see
how i carry home
in paper bags
and phone calls

how
each step forward
leaves footprints
in two soils

heritage

grandfather's hands

built walls

that still stand

in warsaw

mine

type words

in air-conditioned rooms

do

both of us,

somehow,

carry mountains

in our blood?

my office bathroom

in bathroom stalls

between meetings

i press palms

against cold tile

learning how

panic feels

in three-piece suits

some tears

never fall

siesta
_____

between meetings
i find silence
in bathroom stalls

bright lights
making ghosts
of white men
in black suits

we share the secret
of
almost breaking

the rules

they taught me
to want quietly
to hunger politely
to burn within lines

but your hands
know nothing
of should

old ways

uncles ask

why i need therapy

when vodka

and sunday mass

worked for generations

i try

to explain

how healing

speaks

new languages now

lessons

when he asks
what it means
to be a man

i don't talk
about muscles
or silence

instead;
i demonstrate
how to hold
a wound
with both hands

between shifts

beneath lights
i count breaths
like overtime hours

tie loosened
sleeves rolled up
guard finally down

sometimes strength
is letting yourself
be tired

sunday afternoon

sunlight filters

through dusty blinds

painting tiger stripes

across my father's chair

empty now

except for memories

of how he'd sit here

in rare quiet moments

showing me

without words

that warriors too

need rest

playing catch

you threw
the baseball
high enough
to touch clouds

i'm still learning
how to catch
things that fall
from heaven

evening

starved

haven't been
held in months

skin forgetting
the language of
gentle things

hips forgetting
the motion of
ungentle things

were I fed
i might not have died

sessions

my hands remember

every fight

they never started

healing comes

in whispered stories

to a stranger

who teaches me

how to hold pain

like water

on crying

my therapist says
it's okay to cry

but my throat
still remembers
how father's voice
broke
that one time

and never again

the train ride

city lights blur
through windows
like memories
i can't touch

while strangers
avoid eye contact
with their own
reflections

i count stations
until home
is promised

the artists' studio

paint dries

differently

and canvas

can hold

a secret

as well

as skin

the cat in a bowl

washing dishes in half-light

her cat watches me

from its glass bowl

we share

in silence

things

left undone

stage notes

i played the part

they wanted:

strong jaw

straight spine

silent words

until the script

grew heavy

as chainmail

now i learn

the freedom of improv

and suffer

for it

undoing

first
i had to break
my own rules

untie the knots
of who i should be

until my hands
remembered
how to
hang softly

a bridge

culture

is not a wall

but a river

we are always

crossing

always

becoming

first date

you asked me
what i was afraid of
and i almost told you
the truth:

that your tenderness
terrifies me
more than my anger
ever could

peeling fruit

peeling fruit
in darkness

juice running
between fingers
like secrets

the way you watch
makes me forget
about napkins

dinner table math

calculating tip percentages

while you decide

if i'm worthy

of another encounter

my worth measured

in dollars

and feet

under the light

fluorescent lights

make ghosts

of us all

evening's prayer

the sun sets

in red confession

birds

carry secrets

past my window

does darkness

hold us

all

this gently?

tending flames

these days
i build fires
in stone circles

each spark
a question

some nights
i watch embers
float like prayers
to dark skies

remembering how
warmth returns

even to cold hands

even to burnt fingers

there is wisdom

in this filtered

light

i am learning

the difference

between

burning

and becoming.

hello, ms patricia

the cleaning crew
knows my name
now

her mop
whispers across tile
like rosaries

some prayers
wear orange suits

circle

they tell us to

sit in circles

to

share stories

and hold

our oldest toys

men learning

how to be soft

with broken things

including

ourselves

stoned-faced

they taught me
protocols
and procedures

how to be stone
in a storm

how to be fire
in a war

how to be guardian
to their streets

but never

how to cry

without

becoming less

of

who they need

bright, light, city

from my balcony

the city wears

its evening face

a thousand windows

bright

with other people's lives

sometimes loneliness

is just

a way to belong

night
_____

hospital waiting

the doctors beep

in expensive codes

while nurses

wear midnight

like armor

some prayers

come

with coffee stains

surname

practicing pronunciation

in midnight mirrors

trying

to make my father's name

fit between my teeth

perhaps

piotr is nothing more

than peter

last train

we ride

in separate seats

neither sleeping

neither speaking

the city rocks us

through darkness

like children

it cannot soothe

night shift

brewing coffee
at 1 AM

like a rebellion
against
tomorrow's
authority

some control
is better
than none

gym mirror

in light
my reflection
grows stronger
than my father's
ever was

but
it still trembles
at raised voices

closing time

walking home
past closed shops
and sleeping cars

even my shadow
seems more honest
at this hour

worker's hands

these calluses

come from

generations

of men

who built

things

yet still shake

when holding

photographs

of home

i love her, still

when the evening blue

bleeds into black

i remember

(quietly)

how i love you

still

permission

sometimes

i want to be

small enough

to hold

to shrink

into corner spaces

where

the world can't find me

but that potion

is only

for Alice

in my father's kitchen

at midnight

i find him here

stirring memories

into soup

we don't speak

of tears

or tomatoes

but both

season the broth

some lessons

come in silence

conversations

wordless conversations

glowing in

cellphone light

know

truths

that daylight

doesn't dare

a view from the roof

city lights

below

like

fallen constellations

counting stars

and satellites

until dawn

admits me back to earth

night prayer

in darkness
i recite
old country
wisdom:

be strong
be silent
survive

but now
i add
my own verses:

be soft

be seen

become

strawberry

you eat strawberries

like they owe you

nothing

while i learn

how desire

ripens

waiting

between time zones
i count hours
backwards to warsaw

while babcia's candles
burn
in my window
like prayers

some nights
even strong men
need blessing

night mass

in empty churches
at midnight
i kneel like father
taught me

but confess
in english
to ghosts
who don't know
my saints

typing

typing
deleting
typing again

how many hearts
died in the space
between
send and unsend

gaming
_____

headset static

crackles with voices

from different time zones

we fight dragons

together

while avoiding talk

of taxes

and divorces

or affairs

and peace

or love

and war

About the Author

Leo Piotr is a Polish-Canadian poet whose work explores the intersection of masculine identity, cultural displacement, and emotional authenticity.

Born in Poland, but raised and living in Toronto, his poetry navigates the spaces between worlds – old and new, strength and tenderness, tradition and transformation.

"The Soft Hours" is his debut collection.